TOMORROW'S TECHNOLOGY

SPACE
NOW AND INTO THE FUTURE

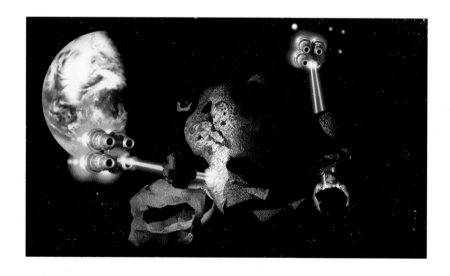

IAN GRAHAM

ILLUSTRATED BY ALEX PANG

Thameside Press

U.S. publication copyright © Thameside Press 1999

International copyright reserved in all countries.
No part of this book may be reproduced in any
form without written permission from the publisher.

Distributed in the United States by
Smart Apple Media
123 South Broad Street
Mankato
Minnesota 56001

Produced for Thameside Press by Bender Richardson White
Project editor Lionel Bender
Project production Kim Richardson
Designer Ben White
Text editor Clare Oliver
Illustrations Alex Pang
Consultants Steve Parker and Virginia Whitby
Picture researchers Cathy Stastny and Jane Martin

Printed in Singapore

ISBN: 1-929298-41-2
Library of Congress Catalog Card Number: 99-71373

Words in **bold** appear in the glossary on pages 30-31.

CONTENTS

INTRODUCTION

Thousands of years ago, people learned the patterns of the **stars** well enough to steer a ship by them. Today, we explore our corner of the **universe** by sending machines into space. In the future, we may live and work in space, or on another planet. Our adventures in space are only just beginning.

WHAT IS SPACE LIKE?

Most of space is empty. Gases and solid particles join together in clumps, making up the Sun, the planets and their **moons**, **asteroids**, **comets**, and other stars. The area between these clumps is empty. There is no air in space and there is little or no **gravity** or heat, unless you are near a star or planet.

WHY TRAVEL INTO SPACE?

As soon as the technology for space travel was developed, people went into space to explore it. Discoveries made in space help us to understand more about how the universe works. In future, we may travel to other planets and moons to mine valuable materials. One day, we may even fight wars in space.

▷ FUTURE TREND

Predicting the future is very difficult. A new invention may be in daily use in five years' time, or it may be delayed for 30 years. It may never happen at all. What is certain is that technology develops all the time. *Future Trend* looks at new developments, which may happen in 20, 40, or even 60 years. They may seem impossible to us today, but for people 50 years ago, so were space satellites.

Space shuttle *Discovery* blasts off from the Kennedy Space Center, Florida. Space shuttle missions include carrying **satellites** into space so they can go into **orbit** around the Earth.

SPACECRAFT

Humans evolved to live on the **Earth**'s surface, not in space. An unprotected human being in space would die in seconds. So, we have to take Earth-like conditions with us. Spacecraft and spacesuits are designed to supply the air and warmth that we enjoy on Earth. They do not provide gravity, the force that holds us down on the Earth's surface, but that is because we are able to do without gravity more easily than without air.

At first, only specially trained, fit, young military pilots were allowed into space. When spacecraft were big enough to carry larger crews, scientists were sent too. In the future, more and more people will have the opportunity to experience a spacewalk, or EVA (extravehicular activity), and view the Earth as it appears from space.

Exploration of space solves many mysteries —and creates new ones. The *Hubble* telescope has sent back pictures of "star nurseries," called **nebulae**, such as the Great Orion Nebula shown here. Nebulae are vast clouds of **matter** in deep space, from which stars are born.

THE SPACE AGE

At the height of the **Cold War** between the former Soviet Union and the United States, the Soviets launched the first artificial satellite, *Sputnik 1*, on October 4th, 1957. It was the start of the **space age**. A month later, *Sputnik 2* carried the first living creature, Laika the dog, into space. Then on April 12th, 1961, Yuri Gagarin blasted off in *Vostok 1* to become the first person to orbit the Earth. The space race had begun.

RACE TO THE MOON

In 1961, President Kennedy announced that an American would stand on the Moon by 1970. The U.S. space agency, NASA, set about testing spacecraft and techniques to land people on the Moon and bring them back. During six one-man *Mercury* spaceflights from 1961 to 1963 and ten two-man *Gemini* flights from 1965 to 1966, astronauts practiced changing orbits, finding other spacecraft, and docking with them.

Earth

6

STAGED ROCKETS

A **rocket** is really two or three rockets, called **stages**, standing on top of each other. Each stage contains tanks full of **fuel** and **oxidizing agent**. The oxidizing agent helps the fuel to burn and is either pure **oxygen**, or a chemical rich in oxygen. The first stage lifts the rocket off the ground. When its tanks are empty, the stage is dropped to save weight. The next stage fires, and the next, until the rocket reaches a speed of 17,000 m.p.h. and goes into orbit.

▶ FUTURE TREND

SPACE PIRATES?

One day, space travel will become as commonplace as travel by sea is today. There may even be space pirates. They would cruise through space in search of craft carrying cargoes of precious minerals. If this happened, space police would be needed. They would patrol the solar system and protect cargo spaceships. The police would have the power to stop suspicious-looking spacecraft and search them for stolen goods.

THE FIRST MOON LANDING

Gemini prepared the way for a Moon mission. The three-man *Apollo* spacecraft was made in modules that could separate from each other. One astronaut circled the Moon in the command and service module (CSM), while the other two landed in the lunar module (LM). *Apollo 11* touched down in July 1969, just within President Kennedy's deadline. Neil Armstrong was the first man on the Moon. In all, 12 *Apollo* astronauts visited the Moon between 1969 and 1972.

The rocket that carried *Apollo 11* into space was called *Saturn 5*, which had three stages. Here, *Saturn* drops its used-up second stage.

AN APOLLO MISSION

1 CSM and LM head for the Moon
2 CSM releases LM and orbits the Moon
3 LM lands
4 LM takes off
5 LM joins waiting CSM
6 CSM returns to Earth

Moon

1

2

3

4

5

The LM lands safely. Wearing backpack units that contain oxygen supplies, the astronauts step out to collect precious samples, take photos and set up scientific equipment.

Their mission complete, the astronauts leave behind any heavy equipment and use the LM's landing stage as a launchpad. In the lift-off stage, they rocket up to meet the waiting CSM.

To bring astronauts safely back to Earth, **capsules** were fitted with parachutes, which slowed down the descent. Even so, landing on hard ground could cause serious injury. Many manned capsules were designed to splash down in the ocean instead. These capsules carried inflatable air bags to keep them afloat until the astronauts were rescued.

SPACEPLANES

When you fly somewhere on vacation, the airline would be crazy to use the plane for one flight and then throw it away. But that is what space agencies have to do with their super-expensive rockets. The first reusable spacecraft, the space shuttle *Columbia*, did not make its first flight until April 12th, 1981.

SHUTTLING INTO SPACE

The United States began experimenting with a rocket-powered spaceplane called the *X-15* in 1959. In nine years, the strange, pencil-thin plane with short, stubby wings made almost 200 flights to the edge of space, but it could not go into orbit or it would have melted during reentry. Lessons learned from flying the *X-15* were used to help design the space shuttle. With its two rocket boosters and external fuel tank, the space shuttle can carry up to seven astronauts and more than 30 tons of cargo in its payload bay. Today NASA operates a fleet of four shuttles—*Columbia*, *Discovery*, *Endeavor*, and *Atlantis*. A fifth shuttle, *Challenger*, was destroyed in an explosion 73 seconds after takeoff on January 28th, 1986, with the loss of all seven of its crew.

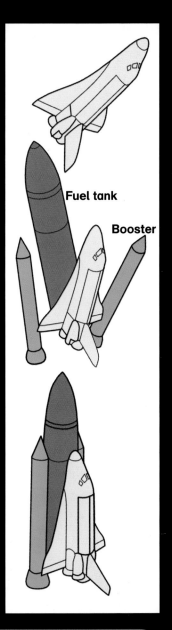

Fuel tank

Booster

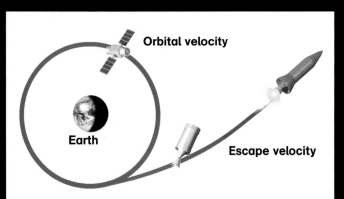

Orbital velocity

Earth

Escape velocity

The space shuttle releases its boosters and spent fuel tank as it ascends. The slim boosters are retrieved and reused.

At orbital velocity, a spacecraft travels ten times faster than a bullet. Escaping orbit requires even greater speed.

▷ FUTURE TREND

AWAY-DAYS TO ORBIT?

Some time next century, passenger spacecraft will be able to take off from an ordinary airport. You settle back in your seat as the plane lifts off. Instead of it heading for a sun-drenched vacation resort, its nose tips up and it flies straight upward, because this is a spaceliner. Less than ten minutes after takeoff, your personal stereo floats past your face. You are in orbit. Traveling in space you could circle the Earth in one hour.

21ST-CENTURY SPACEPLANES

A new generation of 21st-century spaceplanes are being designed and built right now. One of them is the Lockheed *VentureStar*. It will go one better than the space shuttle. *VentureStar* is a type of spacecraft, called a Single Stage to Orbit craft, that has no add-on bits such as boosters or fuel tanks on the outside. A small prototype of *VentureStar*, called the *X-33*, is being tested to solve technical problems before the full-size spaceplane is built.

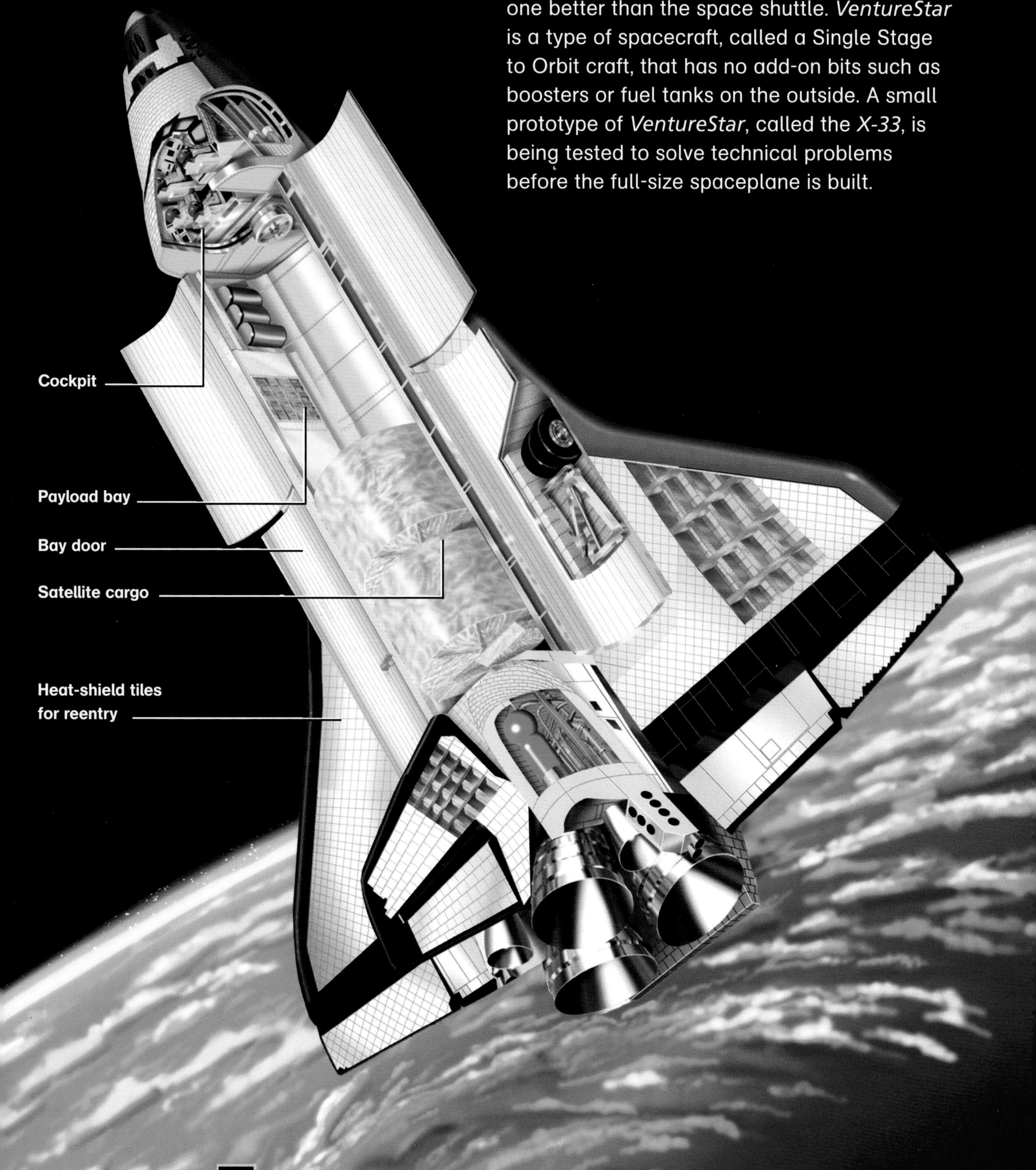

Cockpit

Payload bay

Bay door

Satellite cargo

Heat-shield tiles for reentry

MANNED PLANETARY FLIGHTS

Astronauts are likely to be stepping onto the surface of **Mars** within 25 years. Getting them there will be the most difficult space mission ever attempted—and the longest.

The Moon is always quite near the Earth, on average about 240,000 miles away. Mars' distance varies from 35 million miles to 250 million miles (when it is on the opposite side of the Sun from Earth). At its closest, Mars is a six-month journey away. Astronauts will probably stay on the planet's surface for about two years, so the whole trip could take three years from launch to landing back on Earth.

LIVING ON MARS

The astronauts will have to take three years' supply of food to Mars with them, although they may try to grow some vegetables there to make their diet more interesting. The food will be dehydrated (dried), to make it as light as possible. Water is so heavy that a three-year supply could not be taken. Instead, the astronauts will make all the water they need. The Martian **atmosphere** is mostly **carbon dioxide**. Adding **hydrogen** to it will produce water to drink and to add to food.

On July 4th, 1997, *Mars Pathfinder* landed in this rocky landscape on Mars. Its **solar**-powered rover, *Sojourner*, took photographs and readings for scientists on Earth.

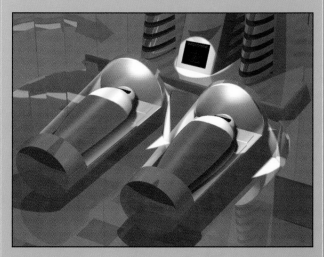

▷ FUTURE TREND

DEEP SPACE TRAVEL?
Spaceflights to the outer planets and especially to the stars will take so long that spacecraft crews may have to be put in the "chiller" between launch and arrival. Crew members are cooled in **cryogenic** chambers for years to keep them in "suspended animation," a sort of human hibernation. Then, the temperature in the chambers will be raised slowly.

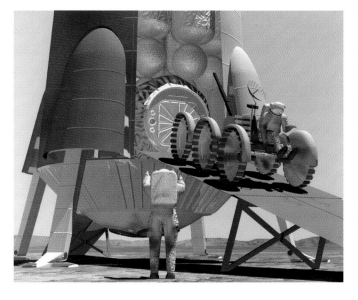

JUST LIKE HOME

There may come a time when the astronauts want to make Mars their home—if a terrible disaster happened on Earth, for example. Bacteria could be used to add oxygen to the atmosphere, making it possible for people to breathe the air and grow plants outside. Huge mirrors could be placed in orbit around the planet to reflect more sunlight onto the poles. This would release the carbon dioxide that is frozen there, making it possible to create a more plentiful water supply. Making a planet more Earth-like is called **terraforming**.

 All the equipment that astronauts need for their stay on Mars will probably be sent to the planet ahead of them. The first flights will take equipment including a nuclear electricity generator and two rover vehicles for getting around on the planet's surface. The astronauts will not blast off from Earth until the equipment reports back that it is working correctly.

Astronauts will carry out scientific research and experiments inside special pressurized containers.

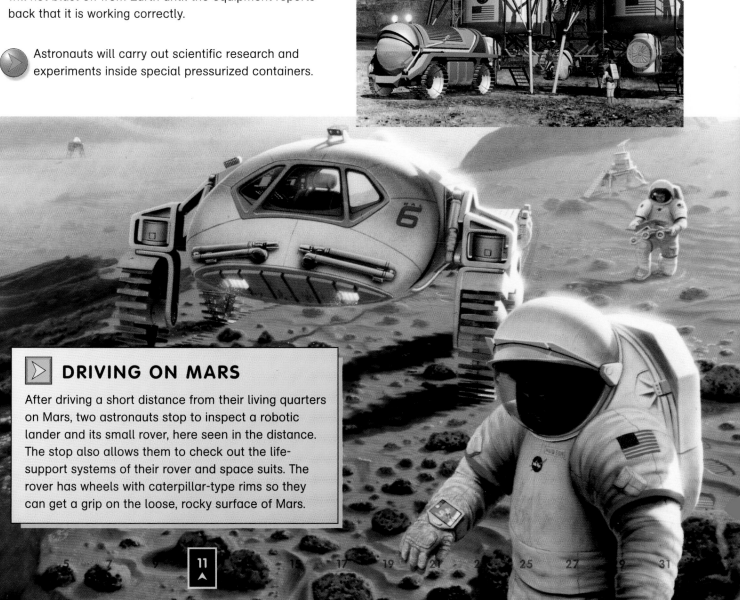

▷ DRIVING ON MARS

After driving a short distance from their living quarters on Mars, two astronauts stop to inspect a robotic lander and its small rover, here seen in the distance. The stop also allows them to check out the life-support systems of their rover and space suits. The rover has wheels with caterpillar-type rims so they can get a grip on the loose, rocky surface of Mars.

SPACE STATIONS

Most manned spacecraft go into space for a short time and then return to Earth. A **space station** stays in space for its whole working life. Different crews visit it and return to Earth, to be replaced by other crews. The station is like a giant floating laboratory. On board, scientists use weightlessness to grow unusual crystals or to understand animals and plants in new ways.

 In 2001 the *Japanese Experiment Module* (*JEM*) will dock with the **International Space Station** (*ISS*). *ISS* will be the biggest structure ever built in space, with parts contributed by 16 countries. From the launch of the first module in 1998, *ISS* should take five years and 45 launches to complete.

STAGING POSTS

A space station also enables scientists to study the Earth and space. The station's crews are studied too, to see how very long spaceflights affect them. In future, a space station could be used as a staging post, where astronauts and spacecraft are prepared for flights to the Moon or to another planet.

MIR SPACE STATION

The Russian space station *Mir* was launched in 1986. It was enlarged by adding extra modules and solar panels to it. Some of its crew members have stayed on board for a year or more at a time, to test the effects of long spaceflights on the human body and mind. *Mir* has suffered power cuts, computer failures, fires, and even a collision with another spacecraft. It survived them all. Coping with these problems has taught scientists and engineers a great deal about how to build new space stations.

▷ FUTURE TREND

SPACE TOURISM?
Wherever explorers and scientists go, tourists follow sooner or later. Japanese engineers have their sights on opening a hotel for space tourists. They have already designed a 550-ton ferry to take tourists to their space hotel. It could also take tourists on orbital tours. To ensure that everyone gets value for money on this trip of a lifetime, the ferry is specially designed to give every passenger a window seat.

MAKING GRAVITY

Weightlessness can be fun, but spending a long time in orbit can make you weak. Muscles and bones waste away if they do not have anything to push against. At the moment, space station inhabitants have to do exercises to stay healthy. In the future, space stations like this one will be made to rotate, creating a **centrifugal force** to replace gravity. You can create centrifugal force by whirling an object on a string around your head— the force pushes the object outward away from you.

STEPS TO REALITY

- NASA has plans to carry empty shuttle fuel tanks, 102 feet long and 26 feet wide, into orbit.

- These empties, joined end to end in a large circle, could be converted into living quarters for 200 people.

- A Japanese construction company estimates that adding central spokes, a power plant, and other vital life-support systems would take just two years.

SATELLITES

Satellites have become very important in our lives. A weather forecaster can predict tomorrow's weather because photos taken by satellites show weather systems developing. A tiny handheld radio receiver can pinpoint someone's position anywhere on Earth by using signals transmitted by satellites. We can watch television programs beamed into our homes from satellites. Cameras and scientific instruments carried by satellites watch the Earth and the stars, increasing our knowledge of the universe.

COMMUNICATIONS SATELLITE

COMMUNICATIONS SATELLITES

We move more information than ever before—and we move it faster than ever before. The first commercial satellite, *Telstar*, was launched in 1962 to transmit TV signals across continents. Its first broadcast lasted just 20 minutes. Today, communications satellites are constantly relaying telephone calls, radio and television programs, and computer data around the world at the speed of light.

NAVIGATIONAL SATELLITE

Satellites vary in size and shape depending on the job they do in orbit. Navigational satellites act as beacons in the sky for ships and airplanes to steer by. Other satellites look outward to study stars and other deep-space objects.

WEATHER SATELLITE

◁ SOLAR POWER

Only a tiny fraction of the Sun's energy reaches the Earth and most of this is either reflected or absorbed by the Earth's atmosphere. Huge solar panels in space could capture more of this solar energy and beam it down to Earth. This energy could be turned into pollution-free electricity and help to reduce our dependence on coal, oil, and gas.

REMOTE SENSING

Gathering information from a distance using a satellite is called remote sensing. Satellite sensors can zero in on just **infrared** or **ultraviolet** rays. They can bounce **radio waves** off the Earth. In these different ways, satellites can spot different types of plants and rocks. They can tell the difference between towns, farmland, and countryside for mapmakers.

FORECASTING THE WEATHER

Weather satellites constantly scan the Earth, looking at the weather systems moving across its surface. They can provide early warning of hurricanes as these head for land. During the day they send television pictures back to Earth. At night, they use heat-sensitive infrared cameras, because the different temperatures of the land, sea, and clouds stand out more clearly in "heat pictures."

FUTURE TREND

OUT OF CONTROL?
When a satellite breaks down, it usually falls silent and becomes a dead hulk in space. But other types of failures are possible. A satellite's computer control system could go haywire and command its thrusters or main rocket motor to fire, sending the craft careering around its orbit out of control. As it twists and turns, stresses beyond its designed strength could splinter the craft into pieces. Worse still, the **space debris** so caused could collide with other satellites and cut vital communications links.

GEOSTATIONARY ORBIT

Communications satellites are placed in a special orbit, known as a geostationary orbit, 22,000 miles above the Equator. Each satellite circles the Earth at the same speed as the planet turns, staying over the same spot on Earth. So once a satellite dish is pointing at the satellite, it never has to be moved.

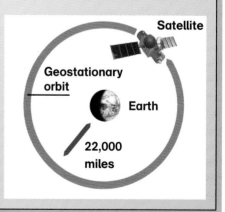

Satellite

Geostationary orbit

Earth

22,000 miles

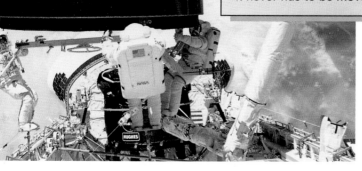

Astronauts from *Endeavor* grapple an *Intelsat VI* communications satellite and maneuver it into their cargo bay. Repairing satellites in space saves the huge expense of launching a replacement.

SPACE PROBES

People have traveled only as far as the Moon, but robot spacecraft have crossed the vastness that lies between Earth and the planets, and beyond. **Space probes** have changed our view of the **solar system**. They proved that there are no intelligent beings living on Mars, that **Venus** is not a beautiful, sunlit planet, and that the moons of the outer planets are not dull, dusty chunks of rock.

TOUR OF THE PLANETS

In 1977, *Voyager 1* and *Voyager 2* left Earth to study the outer planets. As they flew past each planet, they used its gravity to swing them round toward the next planet. The planets lined up in just the right positions to make this possible. Without this help from the planets, the probes could never have carried enough fuel to make the journey.

Voyager 1 reached **Saturn** in 1980 and then left the solar system. *Voyager 2* went on to fly past **Uranus** in 1986 and **Neptune** in 1989 before it too left the solar system. The *Voyagers* took breathtaking close-up photographs of these distant planets.

Sun   Mercury   Earth   Venus   Mars   Jupiter   Saturn   Uranus   Neptune   Pluto

MISSION TO SATURN

In 2004, the *Cassini-Huygens* space probe will arrive at the beautiful ringed planet Saturn. Weighing 6.6 tons, it is the largest deep-space probe ever launched. On arrival, it will split into two probes. *Cassini* will orbit Saturn while *Huygens* investigates Saturn's largest moon, Titan. *Huygens* will plunge into Titan's atmosphere, taking measurements all the way down to the surface. If it survives the landing, it will test the surface.

Cassini was launched in 1997. It is designed to survey Saturn's surface, its rings, moons, and magnetic fields. This task will take the probe about three years to complete.

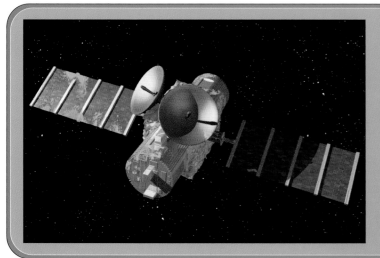

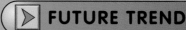

FUTURE TREND

SPACE IVY?
Life may exist in the universe in many different forms. One day, a deep-space probe sent from Earth may encounter an unexpected form of alien life. A parasitic, amoebalike mass of living matter could engulf the probe, scavenging anything it can consume as food. As it grows, it covers the whole probe, as ivy covers a house. When controllers on Earth lose contact with the probe, they might assume it has suffered a technical failure, unaware that it has become an alien snack!

THE GALILEO PROBE

The *Galileo* space probe was launched in 1989 to explore the giant planet **Jupiter**. It was named after the Italian astronomer who discovered Jupiter's moons in 1610. On its way to Jupiter, *Galileo* also took the first close-up photographs of two asteroids, Gaspra and Ida. It discovered that Ida has its own moon, which was named Dactyl. In 1995, *Galileo* became Jupiter's first artificial satellite. It dropped a small probe into Jupiter's stormy atmosphere and went on to explore two of Jupiter's moons, Europa and Io.

Probes that go into orbit around a planet—this is *Cassini* orbiting Saturn—have to perform delicate maneuvers. They have to slow down to match the planet's orbital velocity.

ALIEN LIFE FORMS?

Space probes often make surprising discoveries. For example, scientists now believe Europa is the most likely other habitat for life in the solar system. When probes land on the moons of the outer planets, what might they find? If intelligent beings have ever visited, they may have avoided the hot, inner planets, including Earth, and headed for a moon circling an outer planet. How long will it be before a deep-space probe discovers signs of an ancient landing site?

The *Huygens* probe will take two-and-a-half hours to parachute down through Titan's thick atmosphere. It is designed to survive landing on land or sea—no one knows what it will find.

ASTEROIDS AND COMETS

Pieces of rock and ice left over from the creation of the solar system still orbit the Sun today as asteroids and comets. Asteroids are pieces of rock that differ from the planets only in size—asteroids are smaller. Most asteroids orbit the Sun between Mars and Jupiter. Two small groups of asteroids called the Trojans follow the same orbit as Jupiter, one ahead of Jupiter and the other behind it. Comets are lumps of rock and ice. If a comet flies close to the Sun, some of the ice melts, and gas and dust are given off as bright tails.

Dust tail ——————

Nucleus

Coma

Hydrogen cloud

THE ORIGIN OF COMETS

Scientists think that millions of comets orbit the Sun at a distance of some six million million miles. This is 50,000 times farther than the distance between the Sun and the Earth—too far away for us to see them. From time to time, a nearby star tugs a comet into a different orbit that sends it closer to the Sun. These are the comets that we see.

Although the asteroid belt runs through a huge area of the solar system, each asteroid is widely separated from the next one. Massed together, all the asteroids in the solar system would still weigh less than the Moon.

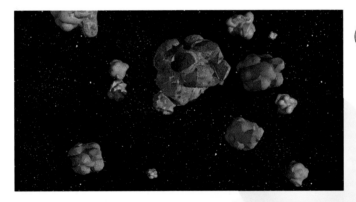

As a comet's orbit draws close to the Sun, the comet develops huge glowing tails of dust and gas. These are blown outward away from the Sun by **solar winds**, sometimes for many thousands of miles.

▷ FUTURE TREND

DODGING ROCKS?

The largest comets and asteroids are tracked by radar. Some of them pass close to the Earth. One day, scientists may detect a comet or an asteroid that is on a collision course with the Earth. A serious impact could have catastrophic results. But the scientists of the future may have the technology to prevent the disaster. Space cruisers could fire powerful missiles at the comet, so that their explosions would push it safely off course and away from the Earth.

THE EARTH'S SCARS

Most of the signs that large objects have hit the Earth in the past have been destroyed by wind and weather. But in the state of Arizona, there is the unmistakable shape of an impact **crater**. The shallow pit of Meteor Crater is 4,000 feet across and 590 feet deep, with a 200-foot high rim. It was made between 5,000 and 50,000 years ago, when a 330-foot wide iron **meteorite** slammed into the Earth.

_____ **Gas tail**

This telescope image of the comet Hale-Bopp shows its two tails. The tail that appears blue is made of gas; the yellower tail is made of dust particles. Hale-Bopp passed near the Earth in 1997. The comet was first discovered in 1994 by two amateur astronomers, Alan Hale and Thomas Bopp.

GREAT BALLS OF FIRE

On June 30th, 1908, a huge explosion ripped through the sky over a remote part of Siberia, Russia, above the River Tunguska. The giant fireball was clearly visible from villages and towns about 500 miles away. The impact of the fireball striking the ground had 1,000 times the power of the Hiroshima atomic bomb. When scientists eventually reached the spot, an extraordinary sight met their eyes. They found 770 square miles of flattened trees. Scientists think that a comet weighing between 100,000 and 1,000,000 tons hit the Earth's atmosphere at 60,000 m.p.h. The air around the comet could have reached temperatures as high as 27,000°F. The intense heat would have vaporized the comet before it reached the ground.

▷ DINO DESTRUCTION?

A catastrophic collision between an asteroid and the Earth may explain the mysterious disappearance of the dinosaurs. Scientists have found evidence that a 6-mile wide asteroid crashed off the coast of Mexico 65 million years ago. The explosion caused fires, giant waves, and endless winter, as billions of tons of dust blocked out the Sun. Climate change may already have been making life difficult for the dinosaurs. The impact probably wiped them out.

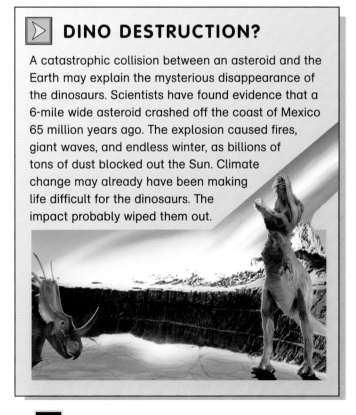

SPACE MINING

When people go to live on the Moon and on Mars, they may not have to take everything they need all the way from Earth. They may be able to use what they find around them to make building materials, rocket fuel, and even oxygen to breathe. And when some of the raw materials that we use here on Earth begin to run out, we may be able to look beyond the Earth for new supplies.

RESOURCES

The inner planets—Mercury, Venus, Earth, and Mars—are covered by volcanic rocks rich in iron and magnesium. The surface of Mars is rich in iron.

The atmospheres of the outer planets —Jupiter, Saturn, Uranus, Neptune, and Pluto—are an almost limitless source of gases such as **helium**, **methane**, **ammonia**, and hydrogen. Large quantities of water-ice lie on some of the moons of Jupiter and Saturn.

Pluto

Neptune

Uranus

Saturn

Earth

Mars

Venus

Mercury

Moon

Jupiter's moons

Jupiter

FUEL ON THE MOON

Scientists think there could be as much as 300 million tons of ice on the Moon. It is lying inside craters near the Moon's poles, where the sunlight casts deep, cold shadows. If this was collected, it could be melted and split into hydrogen and oxygen to use as rocket fuel. The Moon is also rich in a material called helium-3, which is almost unknown on Earth. Scientists believe that helium-3 could be used to make electricity by a process called nuclear fusion. There is enough helium-3 on the Moon's surface to meet all the Earth's energy needs for 700 years. The Moon's crust may also contain many other useful minerals, deposited there by meteorites that have collided with the Moon.

Robot rovers such as *Sojourner* send back useful information to scientists on Earth. The robots can perform simple experiments to test the mineral contents of substances on the surface.

CAPTURING COMETS?
Some of the objects that come close to the Earth may be comets, not asteroids at all. Every time a comet orbits the Sun, it loses tons of dust and gas. Eventually, there is no more to lose and only the rocky core of the comet is left. We could send spacecraft to land on the core and collect any useful minerals and bring them back to Earth. We might even be able to use rockets to divert a comet into orbit around the Earth, or land it on the Moon.

MINING ASTEROIDS
Asteroids are rich in metals such as iron and nickel. The main asteroid belt is 200 million to 280 million miles from the Earth, but some asteroids come much closer to the planet. They could be mined by sending automatic spacecraft to land on them. A spacecraft could be studying a near-Earth asteroid called Nereus as early as the year 2002, in preparation for a later mining mission. The technology used to mine asteroids might also be able to deflect asteroids that are traveling on a collision course with Earth.

◁ PLANET FUEL

The outer planets of the solar system are giant gas balls made mostly of hydrogen, with methane and ammonia. These are very useful gases for making rocket fuel. Tankers could orbit the planets, skimming gas off their outer atmosphere. The gas could be purified, compressed, and stored in tanks.

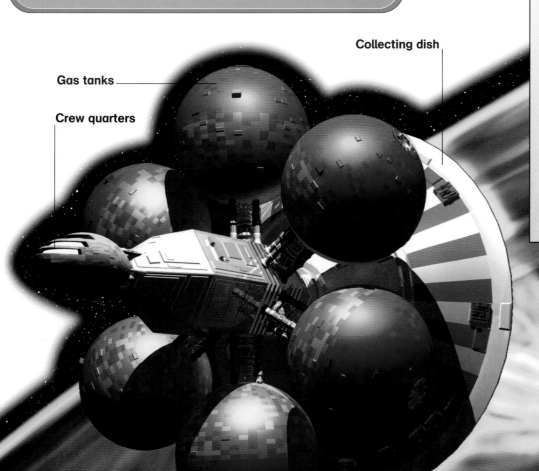

Collecting dish

Gas tanks

Crew quarters

TELESCOPES

Telescopes use lenses and mirrors to make distant objects look bigger and closer. They reveal stars, distant **galaxies**, and nebulae that are too faint to see with the naked eye. But our atmosphere distorts telescope images of the stars. It also stops some of the energy given out by stars from reaching us. One answer is to build telescopes on high mountains, where the air is clearer. Another is to launch them into space, beyond the atmosphere altogether.

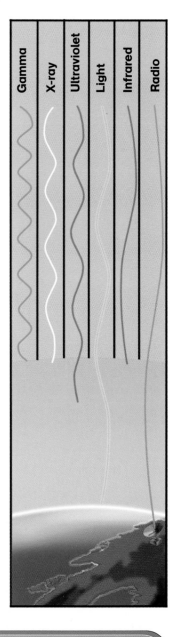

Gamma | X-ray | Ultraviolet | Light | Infrared | Radio

The *Very Large Array* is a set of 27 **radio telescopes** in the New Mexico desert in the United States. These are carefully positioned so that together they act as one giant, powerful dish, picking up even the faintest radio signals.

Telescopes can see with senses that respond to all parts of the electromagnetic spectrum, including **gamma rays**, **x-rays**, ultraviolet, visible light, infrared, and radio waves. All of these are reflected or absorbed by the Earth's atmosphere, except for light and some radio waves.

▷ FUTURE TREND

STARGAZING FROM THE MOON?
Telescope pictures are easily spoiled by stray light or unwanted radio waves entering the telescope. So astronomers have to build their telescopes in more and more remote places. The dark side of the Moon may prove to be the best spot for telescopes of the future. They would be shielded from light and radio interference. As there is no atmosphere on the Moon, viewing conditions are perfectly clear.

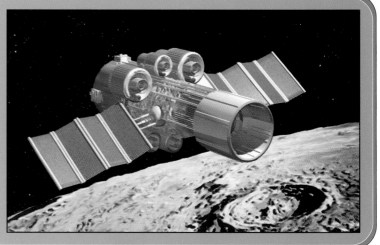

This image of the Pistol Star and Nebula was taken by the *Hubble* space telescope. The nebula is not really this color. *Hubble*'s photos are interpreted by computer.

A VERY LARGE TELESCOPE

The bigger a telescope is, the more light it collects. Collecting more light enables a telescope to see fainter objects. Soon after the year 2000, the world's newest and largest telescope will be completed. The *Very Large Telescope (VLT)* in Chile is not a single telescope but up to seven interconnected telescopes. Four telescopes with mirrors 27 feet across will work together like one telescope with a massive 52-foot mirror. Combined with three smaller telescopes, they will be able to see something as small as a man as far away as the Moon.

A scientist of the future controls a range of Earth-based and space telescopes. Data from the different instruments is combined to give a detailed, 3-D picture.

RADIO TELESCOPES

Radio telescopes detect radio waves. They make radio pictures of the sky. Atoms and molecules in space send out radio waves of certain lengths. Hydrogen atoms, which are very common in space, send out radio waves 8 inches long. Radio telescopes can be tuned in to them. The world's largest radio telescope is 980 feet across and built inside a natural hollow in the ground on the island of Puerto Rico. Called *Arecibo*, this telescope cannot be aimed at objects in space. Scientists have to wait until the Earth's rotation points the dish at the object they want to study.

SPACE TELESCOPES

Telescopes in space can look at the whole range of energy waves given out by stars and planets. Some telescopes look at long radio and infrared waves. Others are sensitive to light, and a few are designed to detect shorter ultraviolet waves, x-rays, or gamma rays. The biggest, the *Hubble* telescope, can detect visible light, ultraviolet, and infrared. It is a reflecting telescope with a main mirror 7.9 feet across that can see objects 50 times fainter than any ground telescope can see.

STAR WARS

Every new development in science and technology is studied to see if it can be used to improve existing weapons or create new ones. Space technology has military uses too. Rockets can carry powerful explosive warheads to their targets faster than the speed of sound. Satellites are used for military communications, gathering information, and detecting enemy missiles. The opening shots of a future war may be aimed at destroying these satellites.

ANTISATELLITE SATELLITES

If satellites have to be destroyed in a future space war, **antisatellite satellites** and missiles will do the job. Antisatellite satellites will orbit high above the Earth, silent and unseen. When commanded from Earth, they will maneuver close to enemy satellites and explode. The explosions will shatter the enemy. Antisatellite missiles fired by fighter planes flying high in the atmosphere will climb into space and head for enemy satellites too.

LASER BATTLE STATIONS

Lasers produce intense beams of energy which can be directed onto a single spot. When a laser beam is aimed at a rocket, it can heat a small point on the shell to such a high temperature that it punches a hole through and ignites the fuel inside. This causes a massive explosion that destroys the rocket. Rockets and airplanes have been destroyed by lasers in tests, but getting laser weapons to work in a real battle may prove more difficult. Powerful lasers are very heavy, so they may not be used in space at all. One answer would be to keep the laser on the ground and project its beams into space. Unfortunately, laser beams are absorbed by moisture in the air, so these space-age weapons would not work if it started raining!

Many of the missiles that will be fired in a future war will fly out into space before dropping back into the atmosphere over their targets. Space weapons will try to destroy them as they rise into space.

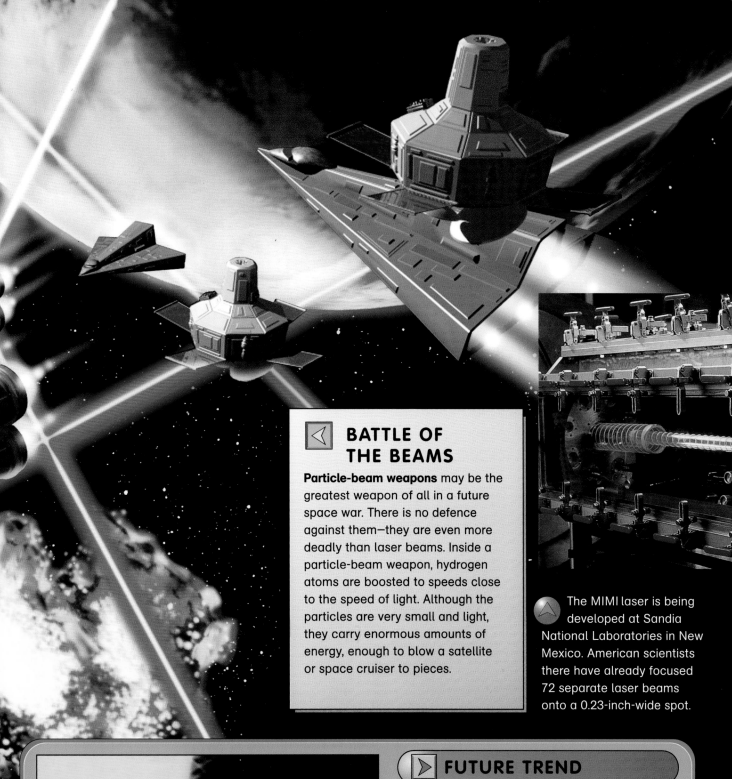

BATTLE OF THE BEAMS

Particle-beam weapons may be the greatest weapon of all in a future space war. There is no defence against them—they are even more deadly than laser beams. Inside a particle-beam weapon, hydrogen atoms are boosted to speeds close to the speed of light. Although the particles are very small and light, they carry enormous amounts of energy, enough to blow a satellite or space cruiser to pieces.

The MIMI laser is being developed at Sandia National Laboratories in New Mexico. American scientists there have already focused 72 separate laser beams onto a 0.23-inch-wide spot.

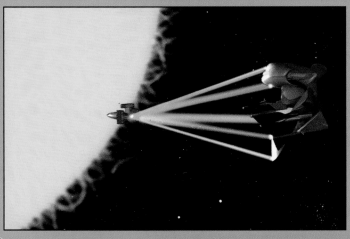

FUTURE TREND

FISHING FOR SPACE JUNK?
Debris and wreckage hurtling about in space is highly dangerous to orbiting satellites and space stations. The U.S. Air Force is already tracking more than 8,500 large pieces of space junk. After a space war, shattered satellites could fill the space around Earth with so much space junk that spaceflight would become impossibly dangerous. If that happened, the scientists of the future might launch vast nets into orbit to catch all the debris and send it toward the Sun.

IS ANYBODY OUT THERE?

While some scientists scan the distant universe for signs of intelligent life, others are looking closer to home. Scientists used to think that the outer planets must be lifeless because they were too far from the Sun. Then a discovery at the bottom of the Atlantic Ocean changed all that. Creatures were found living around springs of superhot water on the seabed where no sunlight ever reaches. Their energy came from heat from the center of the Earth. It seems that life may not need energy from the Sun after all.

Mars Pathfinder used an unusual landing technique. To avoid getting tangled in its parachute, the probe dropped the last few yards wrapped in protective air bags.

CANALS ON MARS

The American astronomer Percival Lowell thought he had seen proof of intelligent life on Mars in the 1890s. He claimed he could see a network of canals that must have been built by Martians, but other astronomers were unable to see them. When the *Mariner 9* space probe took close-up photographs of Mars in 1971, there were no canals. But it did discover channels that looked as if they had been carved out by flowing water. And where water had once flowed, life may have developed. Scientists set about designing a space probe to land on Mars and look for life.

FUTURE TREND

SPEAKING TO ALIENS?
If we found a probe sent by intelligent beings from a distant star system, or picked up an alien message, how should we respond? The alien civilization could be more advanced than we are. They might study us as primitive life forms, as we study laboratory rats!

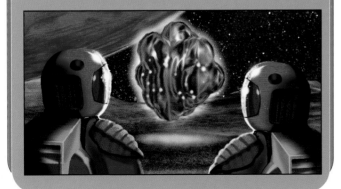

A NEW VIKING INVASION

Two *Viking* spacecraft headed for Mars in 1976. They each split in two. One part orbited the planet and relayed radio signals to Earth from the other section, which landed on Mars. Photographs taken by the landers showed a red, rock-strewn surface. *Viking 2* took photos of water ice forming on the ground during the Martian winter. The landers were equipped with an automatic laboratory to test the soil for life. But although some chemical activity was detected, no life was found.

FOSSILS FROM THE RED PLANET?

Some scientists think they may have found evidence of life on Mars—on Earth. A meteorite found in Antarctica began as a rock from Mars. It was blasted out of the surface of Mars by an asteroid impact hundreds of millions of years ago. It drifted through space for millions of years before it fell to Earth near the South Pole. Inside the rock, scientists found microscopic shapes, smaller than bacteria. Could these be the fossils of ancient Martian life forms?

Olympus Mons on Mars is the largest volcano in the solar system. It is now extinct, but when it was active, lava flowed down its sides and across the Martian surface for up to 2,500 miles, to a depth of over 4 miles in places.

▷ VISIT FROM AN ALIEN

In the movies, alien spacecraft are often shown as flying saucers. But if aliens did come to visit Earth, their craft would probably look unlike anything ever seen by us. Perhaps their craft would be in the shape of a sphere, surrounded by a force field of energy. Alien building materials might include substances unknown on our planet. The energy used to power the craft might be gathered by **solar sails**, or might use new energy sources that we have not yet discovered.

STAR TRAVEL

The stars are so far away that even if we could travel at the speed of light, it would take years to reach the nearest ones. If we are ever going to visit the stars, we will have to invent new ways of traveling much faster than we can now. Chemical rockets are fine for the short hop into Earth-orbit or to the Moon, but for **interstellar** travel they are just too slow.

A POSSIBLE SHORTCUT

Some scientists have proposed amazing ideas for traveling to the stars. Some suggest that it would be easier to bend space itself than to produce a spaceship capable of interstellar speeds. Another theory is that there may be folds in space that bring distant parts of the universe very close together—if only we could find out how to bridge the gap between the folds. The answer may be a **wormhole**, a sort of cosmic tunnel linking two different parts of the universe. Unfortunately, no one has found a wormhole yet, or worked out how to make an artificial one.

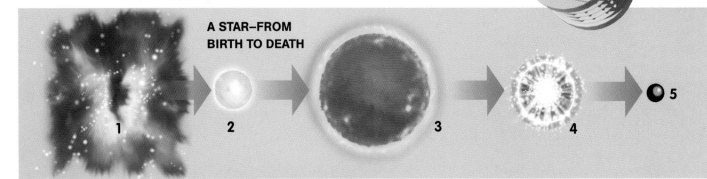

A STAR—FROM BIRTH TO DEATH

1   2   3   4   5

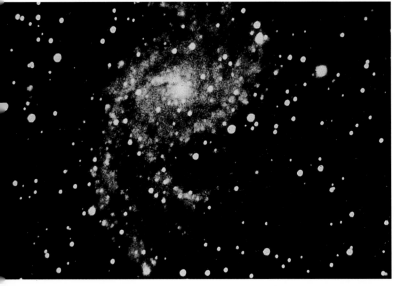

1. A bright young star is born in a dense cloud of gas and dust, known as a nebula.

2. For billions of years, the star shines as a yellow star, slowly becoming hotter and brighter.

3. Eventually the hydrogen fueling the star begins to run out. The star expands and cools into a red giant.

4. The star may lose its outer layers or, if it is very large, explode as a massive **supernova**.

5. At the last stage of its life the star is called a white dwarf. All that remains is its small, hot core.

To reach this galaxy in the constellation of Cepheus, we would need *Star Trek*'s imaginary **warp drive** to boost spacecraft to faster-than-light speeds.

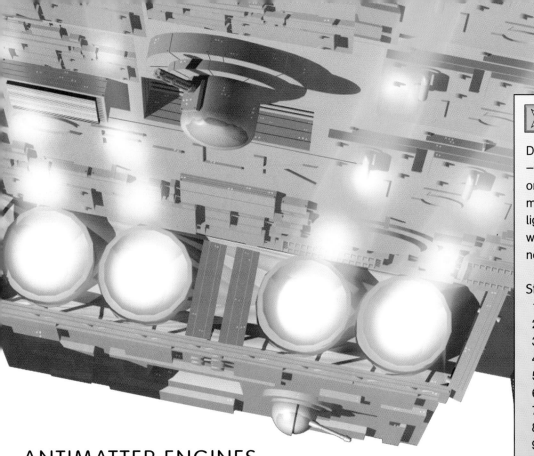

ANTIMATTER ENGINES

Starships in science fiction are often powered by **antimatter** drives. Their energy comes from the violent reaction between matter and its mirror image, antimatter. But antimatter is not just fiction. When it meets matter, there *is* an explosive outburst of energy— 1,000 times more powerful than a nuclear explosion. Scientists have yet to learn how to make antimatter easily and store it safely.

TIME TRAVEL

Most scientists think that the speed of light is the highest speed possible and that light alone can reach this ultimate speed limit. But a handful of scientists think that there may be particles called **tachyons** that travel faster than light, although no one has found any yet. If we could travel faster than light, interstellar travel would be possible, and so, perhaps, would be time travel.

▷ FUTURE TREND

HITCHING A RIDE FROM A BLACK HOLE?
Black holes are the super-dense cores of collapsed stars. Their gravity is so strong that even light cannot escape from them. Black holes may be quite common in the universe. In the future, we might harness the force of black holes for space travel. A spacecraft skirting around a black hole could use the pull of its gravity to boost its own speed—so long as it took care not to fly too close and get sucked in.

GLOSSARY

ammonia A strong-smelling, poisonous gas containing nitrogen and hydrogen.

antimatter Identical to matter, except antiparticles have the opposite electric charge or the opposite magnetic force to particles of normal matter.

antisatellite satellite A satellite weapon designed to destroy other satellites by blowing them up.

asteroid A rock up to the size of a small planet that orbits the Sun. Most are found in a broad belt between Mars and Jupiter.

atmosphere The gases that surround a planet or moon.

black hole An area of space where the pull of gravity is so strong that not even light can escape.

capsule A spacecraft just big enough for one or two people to sit inside.

carbon dioxide A gas made from carbon and oxygen. The main gas in the atmosphere of Venus and Mars.

centrifugal force A force that pushes a spinning body outward.

Cold War The period of political rivalry between the Soviet Union and the United States, beginning after World War II and ending in the early 1990s.

comet An icy rock in orbit around the Sun. As it nears the Sun, it may develop bright tails. Its orbit can take anything from a few decades to 100,000 years.

crater A hollow in the surface of a planet or moon caused when an asteroid, comet, or meteorite hits it.

cryogenics Chilling living things to very low temperatures.

Earth The third planet from the Sun, our home planet, and the only planet known to support life.

fuel A chemical that is burned to provide the energy for an engine to work.

galaxy A collection of stars, dust, and gas moving together through space. The Sun is one of billions of stars in a galaxy called the Milky Way.

gamma rays Invisible waves of energy similar to light, but made from much shorter waves.

gravity The force that pulls everything toward the center of a star, planet, or moon. The more massive a star, planet, or moon is, the stronger its pull of gravity.

helium A light gas made from hydrogen inside stars.

hydrogen The simplest, lightest, and most abundant element in the universe.

infrared Invisible energy waves similar to light, but made from longer waves; also called heat rays.

International Space Station A new space station being built from parts supplied by 16 countries.

interstellar Between the stars.

Jupiter The fifth planet from the Sun and the biggest planet in the solar system.

laser A device designed to produce an intense beam of energy. High-power lasers are used as weapons.

light year A measurement of distance based on how far light can travel in one year.

Mars The fourth planet from the Sun, also known as the Red Planet because of its rust-red colour.

matter The "stuff" that everything is made from—all the particles that make up atoms and molecules.

Mercury The closest planet to the Sun.

meteorite A space rock, or meteoroid, that survives its entry into the Earth's atmosphere and lands.

methane A gas that contains carbon and hydrogen. It can be used as a rocket fuel.

moon A small, natural satellite in orbit around a planet. At least one asteroid has a moon too.

nebula (plural **nebulae**) A cloud of dust or gas in space.

Neptune The eighth planet from the Sun.

orbit The endless circling path of one object around another, due to the force of gravity.

oxidizing agent Oxygen, or a chemical containing oxygen, that enables a rocket's fuel to burn.

oxygen A colorless, odorless gas that we have to breathe in order to live.

particle-beam weapon A weapon of the future that fires a beam of high-speed particles.

Pluto The ninth planet from the Sun. Because of its strange orbit, some astronomers think that Pluto is not a planet at all, but a comet.

radio telescope A telescope that makes maps or pictures of parts of the sky from radio waves.

radio waves Invisible waves of energy similar to light, but with longer waves. Radio waves may be anything from 0.4 inch long to thousands of feet long.

rocket A vehicle that pushes itself through the atmosphere or space by jet propulsion.

satellite An object that orbits another object. The Moon is Earth's natural satellite.

Saturn The sixth planet from the Sun. Saturn is circled by rings made from dust and ice.

solar To do with the Sun.

solar sail A spacecraft propelled by sunlight, by using an enormous sail to catch the solar wind.

solar system The Sun and everything that orbits it—the planets, moons, asteroids, comets, and meteors.

solar wind Particles that escape from the Sun and flow out into space.

space age The time in history since the first artificial satellite, *Sputnik 1*, was sent into space in 1957.

space debris Parts of old rockets and spacecraft that litter space and orbit the Earth.

space probe An unmanned spacecraft sent to study a planet, moon, asteroid, or comet.

space shuttle A reusable spacecraft that ferries cargo and astronauts from the ground to low Earth-orbit.

space station A large spacecraft that stays in space all its working life and is visited by a series of crews.

stage One section of a multistage rocket that has its own fuel tanks and rocket motors.

star A ball of gas so big that hydrogen particles in its center collide and join together to form helium, releasing heat and light.

supernova A huge explosion caused when a massive star collapses and throws off its outer layers.

tachyon A particle that, if it exists, can travel faster than the speed of light.

terraforming Making a planet or moon more Earth-like.

ultraviolet Invisible energy waves similar to light but with shorter waves. Strong ultraviolet light kills living things.

universe Everything there is—every speck of matter, every wave of energy, and all of space.

Uranus The seventh planet from the Sun. It is tipped right over so that one pole faces the Sun.

Venus The second planet from the Sun. Its atmosphere reflects light so well it is often mistaken for a star.

warp drive An imaginary type of spacecraft engine that is capable of faster-than-light travel.

wormhole A tunnel-like shortcut between two places in the universe that are normally a great distance from each other.

x-rays Invisible waves of energy similar to light but with much shorter waves, shorter than four hundred-millionths of an inch.

INDEX